FAITH THROUGH THE FIRE

*A Survival Manual for Those
Who Still Believe God Is Good
When Life Has Been Brutal*

Kia Luster

Dedication

I give honor and glory to God my healer, my keeper, my refuge, and my redeemer. You walked with me through every valley, every fire, and every tear. When I could not stand, you carried me. This book exists because of Your faithfulness. Thank you, LORD, for carrying me through the toughest seasons of my life, for trusting me with the assignments, and for always showing up faithful and strong. Thank you for allowing me to be sensitive to your Holy Spirit for you said that you would not leave me comfortless. Jesus, thank you for being the fourth man in the fire ensuring that the flames did not burn me and that I do not smell like smoke. There's no one greater! Father, I love you, I honor you, and I praise your holy name.

This book is dedicated to my sons, Xavier and Hunter.

You are my reasons for fighting, my motivation for healing and doing the hard work, and my motivation for breaking the generational curses so that you will not have to. Thank you for believing in me when life was hard, as you were watching your mom unravel. God truly blessed me with the best sons a mother could ask for. You are truly my heart in human form, and being your Mommy is my greatest joy. You walked through the fire with me, and we came out unscathed. I love you with my entire being.

To My Husband

Thank you for walking through the fire with me, even when we had to walk apart for a season. Our restoration is a testimony of God's grace, mercy and power. I am grateful for the work God has done in both of us and for the love we now share in Him.

To My Valley Walkers

My sisters in Christ who interceded for me, cried with and for me, and covered me through these difficult seasons without judgment, thank you for loving me through the fire. I thank God for you, and I love you infinitely.

To My Family

To those of you who walked through the fire with us while others went silent, thank you for loving us, interceding for us, and choosing to stand with us in support. I thank God for you, and I love you infinitely. We're born into a family; we don't get to choose, but I would choose you over and again!

To every person who has ever had to trust God when it seems as if you are in the loneliest, darkest, deepest seasons of your life, when nothing makes sense and it feels as if all hope is lost, just know you are not alone-*HE (God) will never leave nor forsake you* (Deuteronomy 31:6).

Foreword

Do you believe in divine connections?

Not the accidental meetings we casually dismiss as coincidence, but the sacred intersections orchestrated by the sovereign hand of God. Moments when heaven quietly arranges what earth could never manufacture. Moments when paths cross not by chance, but by calling.

I believe wholeheartedly that meeting Kia was not coincidence, but providence – an appointment authored by God Himself. I believe holding this book in your hand is a divine connection. A connection to courage, to healing, and to deeper faith forged in fire.

Faith Through the Fire is not merely a testimony. It is a lifeline. It is a survival manual written by someone who has walked through flames that could have easily consumed her, yet she chose to believe God is still good.

Kia does not write from theory. She writes from the ashes of lived experience. From valleys that felt endless. From days and nights that were heavy with questions. From seasons where faith was not polished but raw, shameless, and fiercely clinging to Gods unchanging hands.

This book is for those who have whispered, *"LORD, I believe... help my unbelief."*

It is for the person who loves God but cannot reconcile His goodness with their pain. It is for the one who worships with tears in their eyes. It is for the believer who has endured grief, betrayal, loss, heartbreak, disappointment, silence, and spiritual warfare.

What makes this work so powerful is that Kia walks us through part of her sanctification process. Sanctification is rarely glamorous. It is the daily surrender. The wrestling. The pruning.

The breaking of old patterns. The tearing down of generational patterns; strongholds. It is the slow, faithful work of God conforming us into the image of His Son. And more often than we would like, that transformation comes through pressure.

In Scripture, oil is never produced without crushing. The olive must be pressed before it releases what it carries. Kia carries oil that could only have been produced through pressing.

Oil for healing.
Oil for restoration.
Oil for intercession.
Oil for light in seasons that felt overwhelmingly dark.

The crushing did not destroy her; it revealed what God had already placed within her. What the enemy intended for devastation; God used for consecration. What felt like breaking was, in truth, becoming.

Are you afraid to be pressed?

Allow this book to shift your perspective on the pressing. Allow it to remind you that the weight you feel may not be sent to crush you, but to produce something eternal within you.

Within these pages, you will find not a woman who escaped the fire, but one who endured it and emerged carrying oil.

One of Kia's favorite phrases is "smoke and mirrors." And how often has the enemy relied on exactly that, illusions designed to distort our perception of God's character? Smoke that clouds our vision. Mirrors that magnify our pain and minimize His promises.

May this book steady you in the fire,
May it remind you that God is near.
May the smoke clear, the mirrors fall.
May the noise fade, and you hear His call.

Because...God is still good.

Much love,
Shawntrice Amelia Green

Table of Contents

Introduction

When you pass through the waters, I will be with you; and when you pass through the rivers, they will not sweep over you. When you walk through the fire, you will not be burned; the flames will not set you ablaze. Isaiah 43:2 (NIV)

Faith Through the Fire

There are moments in life that change you forever.

Not slowly. Not gently, but abruptly all at once
One phone call
A diagnosis
Betrayal, grief, death

A truth you never wanted to know, and suddenly, the life you were living no longer exists.

If you are holding this book, chances are you know exactly what I mean. You love God. You believe in HIM. You've prayed, maybe even fasted, and yet... something happened that left you broken, grieving, angry and confused. Maybe you lost someone you loved. Maybe you were betrayed by someone you trusted. Maybe your body failed you. Maybe you learned something so painful in that moment you felt as if it shattered your sense of safety forever.

During it all, you were left asking a quiet but terrifying question:

"God, are you still there... do you even see me?"

I wrote this book for the ones who still believe in God but are tired.

For the ones who still pray, but don't know what to say anymore.

For the ones who have picked up their Bible and don't know where to start reading. For the ones feeling suffocated from overwhelm.

For the ones who still show up to church but carry silent pain in their hearts behind the smiles, words of encouragement, and hugs they extend to others.

I am not writing to you from the vantage point of being on the outside looking in.

I am writing to you as someone who has gone through the fire.

I know what it feels like to love God and still feel crushed by life, to be faithful while grieving, and to trust God while your heart is breaking into a million pieces. To read Scripture through tears, to sit through sermons and not be able to tell anyone what was preached. To be in a room full of people and still feel invisible and alone. To show up and fulfill the roles expected of you, all while feeling empty on the inside. To be running on fumes with your mind in the clouds, to worship with questions, and to cling to hope when everything around you is coming undone.

This book is not about pretending everything is okay.

It is about learning how to stand on God's Word when your very foundation of everything you thought you knew and were has been crushed.

You will not find polished answers here.
You will find honesty, transparency and vulnerability.
You will find Scripture.

You will find a faith that has been tested, stretched and refined by fire.

If you are walking through loss, trauma, betrayal, illness or heartbreak, you are not weak for struggling. You are human, and God is not offended by your pain. He is near to it. *The Lord is close to the brokenhearted and saves those who are crushed in spirit (Psalm 34:18).*

This is your invitation to sit with me in this sacred space, not to rush healing, not to bypass the grief, the pain, the raw emotions, but to discover that even here... God is still good and the fire will not consume you.

PART I

When the Fire Starts

Chapter 1
When Life Stops Making Sense

There is a moment when you realize the life you thought you were living is over.

Not because you chose it.

Not because you were ready, but because something happened that split your world in two, a before and an after.

Before the phone call.
Before the diagnosis.
Before the betrayal.
Before the truth you never thought you would know.

After the unexpected shift... nothing feels the same.

I didn't wake up one morning expecting my faith to be tested the way it was for eight consecutive years. I love God, I believe in HIS word, I trusted HIS promises. I did what I knew to do: prayed, worshiped, and kept going. But then life came with a force I was not prepared for. Loss began stacking on top of loss. Grief found its way into places I didn't even know could ache. Pain became something I carried, not something I visited and as if everything I was walking through wasn't heavy enough, the world itself began to shut down.

We entered COVID-19 March of 2020, a season of fear, sickness, isolation, death and uncertainty. Churches closed, hospitals filled, and families were separated. Grief became something everyone was carrying, even if for different reasons. While the nation was learning how to live six feet apart, some were debating whether to accept a vaccine or not. I was learning how to survive emotionally and spiritually alone. The usual places of comfort were gone. The routines that held me together disappeared, and the weight of what I was facing had nowhere to go.

It felt like the world was on fire and so was my life.

I was still expected to believe in God, show up for others, be a wife, be a mother, lead a team at work, and lead a women's ministry. You know, continue showing up as the strong one - the one with the answers, the one to hold it all together, and the one who does not get to feel, stop, or just be.

That is one of the hardest parts of being a person who loves Jesus. When everything around you is falling apart, everyone still expects you to be *strong*, to *trust God*, to keep going and not break down, and to just press on and smile through it all.

No one really talks about what that feels like. No one tells you how confusing it is to love God while your heart is breaking or how disorienting it is to worship while grieving. How lonely it is to suffer in silence while still showing up for everyone else when no one is showing up for you.

There were moments when I didn't know how to reconcile what I believed with what I was living. I knew the Scriptures, I knew God was faithful, but I also knew I was hurting. I was angry and pretending that I was fine, and no one saw me coming undone.

When life stops making sense, faith stops being theoretical.

It becomes survival.

You start asking different questions:

God, where are You?
Why didn't You stop this?
Do You see me?
Do You care?

These aren't the questions of someone who doesn't believe. Although church folk would make you feel that way. Notice I said church folk and not women and men of God. There's a difference. They are the questions of someone who believes deeply and is in pain. I had to learn that God was and still is not afraid of my questions. He was not offended by my questions or my tears. He was not distant from my confusion. He met me in it.

Not always with answers in that moment, but always with HIS presence. *HE (God) will never leave nor forsake you* (Deuteronomy 31:6).

There is something holy about the place where faith and suffering meet. It is where illusions fall away, where shallow belief dies and where a deeper, truer relationship with God is formed.

If you are in that place right now where life no longer makes sense and faith feels heavy, I want you to know something:

You are not weak.
You are not failing.
You are not abandoned.
You are standing in the fire, and God is still with you.

Chapter 2
Loving God While Being Wounded

Although I was in a place of pain, grief and unanswered questions,

The strangest part of it all was I didn't stop believing in God when my life began to fall apart.

I still prayed.
I still worshiped.
I still read my Bible.
I still taught others about faith, forgiveness, and trusting God, and yet... my heart was breaking.

There is a unique kind of pain that comes when the same God you love is the one you're asking, *"Why?"* It is one thing to be hurt by people. It is another thing to be hurt while you are still holding on to God.

I loved HIM, still, but I didn't fully understand HIM. I trusted HIM, but I was confused, I mean I didn't understand, *"God, why are all of these things are allowed to happen to me,"* but at the same time not wishing this pain on anyone else.

Sometimes, if I'm being honest, I was angry with God.

Not because I stopped believing, but because I believed so deeply that I expected HIM to protect what I loved and to save me from going through the pain of it all.

You see, faith does not make you immune to pain. It makes you feel it more deeply.

When my Daddy died, my marriage was wounded by adultery, my mother in love fell ill and lived with us temporarily so that I could care for her, and my mother came to live with us during this same time. I did not have the opportunity to pause, feel, breathe or just be. While I was carrying everyone else's grief, mines went unspoken. I still showed up in faith spaces, I still ministered, I still encouraged others, I still said, *"God is good"* because HE is, and I have experienced HIS goodness repeatedly in my life.

Yet some days - if I'm honest - those words *"God is good"* felt heavy on my tongue while I was saying them because although I knew it to be true, I did not always feel that way in those moments.

I didn't know how to be both faithful and wounded at the same time. I thought I had to choose: either be strong or be honest, either believe God or feel what I felt. So, I hid.

I hid my questions behind worship.
I hid my tears behind prayer.
I hid my exhaustion behind responsibility. When you love God, sometimes you feel like you don't get to express the emotions and feelings that others would in those situations, but here is what God gently taught me:

Loving Him doesn't mean pretending you're okay.

It means bringing Him what is not. *Cast all your anxiety, on HIM because HE cares for you.* (1Peter 5:7).

God was not asking me to pretend like I had it all together, or that I could carry it all on my own.

HE was asking me to be real with HIM.
HE met me in my confusion.
HE sat with me in my grief.
HE held me in my anger, and HE did not let go when I couldn't make sense of what happened and what was happening.

If you are reading this and you love God, but you are hurting...

If you still pray, but your heart feels tired...
If you still believe, but you don't understand...

You are not a bad Christian.

You are a wounded believer, and God is near to the brokenhearted.

The Lord is close to the brokenhearted and saves those who are crushed in spirit (Psalm 34:18).

Chapter 3
When It's Hard to Breathe

Grief for me didn't come into my life gently. It came in April of 2016, when my Daddy passed away, and with him, a part of my world went silent. As the eldest child, at that moment, I didn't get the luxury of allowing myself to grieve. I became the organizer, the planner, I had to show up as the strong one. The one who made the phone calls, handled the details, and held everyone else together. For clarity, I grew up in what society calls a blended family. I am blessed to have my biological father - my Dad (who is still living and who I have a great relationship with) - and my Daddy (my mother's husband) who raised me from the age of 3 years old. My Dad and Daddy got along quite well. I never felt the pressure to choose, and they surrounded me with so much love.

A couple of months before Daddy passed away, he had a heart-to-heart conversation with me. He told me, in detail, the outline of his funeral services and his concerns for us, his family who would be left behind when he went on to glory (heaven). As my heart was breaking into pieces trying to reconcile what my mind understood was happening because we watched his health decline, I was imagining a world without my Daddy. As I sat in that moment with him, I listened as he gasped for air in between each directive while dependent on oxygen, took note and told him that I would do exactly as he asked. I told myself, *"Be strong Kia. Hold it together. You will deal with the pain and grief later. Right now, you have work to do. You are the eldest, and you have a responsibility to ensure everything is handled and that everyone is ok."*

I will always remember April 15, 2016, the day Daddy passed away, three days before his birthday. The look on my mother's face as my brother, sister and I sat in a conference room at the hospital when I informed the treating physicians that we had made the decision to take him off life support. Everything moved in slow motion as the words left my lips and it was as if my mother's breath was snatched from her body. You see, my parents had been a couple since she was 21, and let's just say Daddy spoiled Mommy, in a good way. Mommy was well loved, wanted for nothing, and was blessed to be married to her best friend and soul mate.

Mommy was in a daze, my brother and sister were hurting, and I was hurting, but I promised Daddy I would be strong, show up for everyone, make and execute the plans, answer all the questions, and hold it all together. But, I was crumbling on the inside. I didn't have time or the space to grieve. Through all the questions, the expectations, the planning, I was screaming on the inside, but no one saw me. *"Kia is so strong,"* I heard family and friends say, but being labeled the "strong one" was not a badge of honor. I loathed hearing it. To me, it felt dismissive of my sorrow. It made me feel unseen and left no space to grieve.

Our children were hurting and watching our reactions, waiting on their Nana (Mommy), my brother, my sister, and I to show them how to navigate life without their Papa.

There was no time to cry. No time to collapse. No space to process what it meant to lose the man who had been such a steady presence in my life - my confidant, my pillar of strength, my example of what a loving husband and father was, the one whose voice brought calm to any situation I faced. My Daddy always knew what to say to bring me back; to center me so I could regroup and keep moving. The one who my husband asked his permission to marry me and poured into my husband on what marriage is and what to expect. Now, he's gone. I loved Daddy deeply, but my grief had to be set aside so I could be what everyone else needed.

Soon after, my mother relocated from Buffalo, New York, to Charlotte, North Carolina, to move in with my Husband, children and me. Mommy was grieving her husband, her best friend, her soul mate, and the one who truly understood her. I listened to and watched her cry, not in the conventional way, but in things she did and choices she made. I comforted her as best as I could and became her anchor to help her navigate her new normal as the spouse of a retired navy veteran and all that came with it so that she could continue living. Still, I held her pain, and I did not grieve my own.

It was as if my heart was placed on a shelf, still there, still beating, but no longer being allowed to feel. Grief has a way of doing that, especially when you are labeled the strong one. People assume you're okay because you look okay. They lean on you because you don't fall, but inside, something begins to tighten. Something begins to ache.

My paternal and maternal grandmothers taught me to *"never allow yourself to look like what you're going through"*. So, I ensured our home was well kept. My hair, nails, appearance was kept up. Business as usual. I didn't realize it then, but my body was already keeping score in every tear I didn't cry. Every hug, every word of encouragement, every smile, every prayer I prayed for someone else instead of myself. For every moment I swallowed my own pain, my body kept record of it all.

Grief doesn't disappear when you ignore it. It waits, and mine was waiting patiently.

PART II

Walking Through the Flames

Chapter 4
The Stranger in My House

Betrayal doesn't announce itself. It arrives quietly through a message, a phone call, a video, a picture, or a truth you never asked for. In June of 2016, two months after my Daddy passed away, a woman reached out to me on social media to tell me she was involved in an affair with my husband. Surely, not my husband. Not the man I took vows with who promised to love me forsaking all others. She must have been mistaken because my husband, the man who I knew him to be, would never. To my dismay, it was true, and when I asked him about it and showed him what she sent to me, he asked if we could go for a walk. There, he told me how it started and that he had already ended it. In anger, she reached out to me to inform me of their affair.

He must have known that in my silence, I was about to swing, because I swung on him, clipping him onto the corner of his jaw, and he quickly stepped back. I turned and walked away because I didn't have the mental or emotional bandwidth to process through or deal with what just happened. All I could think about in that moment was how I wish I could call my Daddy; how badly I needed to hear his voice. But, I couldn't, and honestly, that pained me more than what I had just learned. I knew God was not pleased with how I responded in that moment, and responding in such a manner was so out of character for me. *Oh God, please help me...*

There are moments when the ground shifts under your feet as if the rug you were standing on was snatched right from under you. That was one of them.

I was already exhausted, trying to find a safe place to grieve losing my daddy, already holding everyone else together, and now betrayal in the worst way.

I didn't just feel hurt, I felt humiliated, blindsided, angry, and deeply alone.

Yet even then, I didn't fall apart. I had to put those emotions on the shelf. I did not have the space to feel or process through those emotions.

I still had children to raise and show up for.

A mother to support and a mother-in-love to care for.
A household to run.
A faith to live out in front of others.
A team to lead at work.

So, I went numb.

I tried to pray through it.
I tried to push through it.
I tried to be "strong" through it because that's what's expected from someone who loves Jesus, right?

The thing about betrayal, it cuts differently when it comes from someone who knows your heart. Someone who has access to your vulnerability. Someone you trusted with your life. Someone who watched you go through the motions of losing and having to bury your Daddy. Someone who you took vows with, who you joined in covenant with. You, them and God. Someone who you thought was your best friend.

I had lost all respect for him. I didn't want to hear the apologies, or how sorry he was for his choices and decisions.

I just wanted him gone. I told him I wanted him to go, and it would be easier that way. One less thing to deal with. However, he refused to leave. He wanted to work through it, but to me, there was nothing to work through. I was never the girlfriend who remained after being cheated on because clearly, I was not what they wanted, so I would end the relationship and not look back. Staying with someone who cheated on me was never my ministry. I just didn't understand how I could get back to a good place or even trust the person again.

If I am honest, I was more disappointed in the timing of it than the affair itself. I now had to compartmentalize the affair and put that on a shelf also. I went about my day to day as if he was not even in our home. He was a stranger to me, and I was on auto pilot just going through the motions in the presence of our children and everyone else. But, behind closed doors I had nothing for him. However, once again, *in my silence, my body kept score.*

It was one crisis stacked on top of another. Not long after, my husband was pulled into legal battles with his ex-wife. Court dates, tension, and parental alienation kept our girls from us and fractured our family even further. The blessing is that we have a great relationship with our eldest daughter's mother, and she would come to Charlotte quite often as well as her mom for holidays and events. We, too, are what society calls a "blended family"; both of us previously being married. My husband brought our three beautiful girls who were nine, seven and two when our family began. Our middle and youngest daughter are with his ex-wife. I brought our two boys who were sixteen and four when our family began.

Our children are now twenty-eight, twenty-one, nineteen, sixteen and fourteen. I absolutely love my girls and the relationship we share. I am grateful to God, my husband, and their mothers for the gifts they are. Blending a family is not always easy, but it is worth it. Prayer, patience, love, communication, boundaries and understanding are essential when blending your family.

Our family dynamic may seem unique to some, as our youngest son's father, his family, and I are very close. They embrace my husband and our family as their family also. I love our son's bonus mother, and how she loves our son. We spend holidays, birthdays, cookouts, and game days together.

"Keep moving, Kia" is what I told myself, and so... I kept going.

I smiled in public; showed up at work; showed up at school plays, performances, and sports events as team mom; led a team at work; and led the women's ministry at church.

I taught Scripture.
I spoke about forgiveness.

Inside, though, something was unraveling. I was slowly bursting mentally and emotionally at the seams. I thought I was dealing with it because I was still functioning. However, not facing "it" and processing through what I was carrying was not dealing with "it".

You see, you can forgive and still be wounded. You can pray and still be bleeding. You can love God and still be breaking.

I was learning all of that in real time. Everything I thought our marriage was, it wasn't, and once again, grief was pushed aside.

Cast your cares on the Lord and he will sustain you; he will never let the righteous be shaken (Psalm 55:22).

Chapter 5
When Evil Touches What You Love

There are pains you expect in life and then there are the ones no parent ever prepares for.

In March of 2019, something shifted in my home, not because of something that happened that day, but because of something that had happened years before and was finally spoken out loud.

My eldest son, who was 20 years old at the time, sat down and told me he had been sexually abused starting at the age of 6 years old by someone who had close proximity to our family for 15 years. Someone who had access to him when he was just a small child had violated his safety, his body, and his innocence. He was watching an episode on a talk show where men discussed being abused in their youth and the importance of speaking up and exposing the abuser so that they would not have the opportunity to continue hurting someone else.

I will never forget the weight of that moment. I hugged my son and apologized for not protecting him, for him having to carry this weight and pain for so long on his own, and for not seeing the signs. I told him how proud I was of him for taking back his power and exposing the abuser and the abuse he suffered. We went to the police station, and unfortunately, my son had to relive the abuse all over again as he said what he endured to the detectives during those younger years. *"How did you miss this? A good mother would have known,"* is what I heard the enemy (Satan) whisper into my ear.

Everything inside me broke open - grief, anger, sorrow, disbelief, guilt, shame and a deep, aching love for my child - all at once. It wasn't just the pain of what had happened to him. It was the pain of realizing how long he had carried it alone. I wanted to go back in time. I wanted to protect him in every way I could not back then. I wanted to undo what had been done. I wanted to physically hurt the abuser.

The reality is that I could not go back in time, but what I could do and what I did was believe him, stand with him, and love him without condition. Oh, how I wish I could run to my Daddy's arms, to hear him tell me that it was going to be ok, and to tell me what to do. My mother did not know how to show up for me. She was grieving my Daddy, her life partner, and I could not tell her what I even needed from her. I heard the voice of the enemy whisper in my ear, *"You had one job, Kia! A mother protects her children, and you failed. Maybe your sons are better off without you. You've worked in the mental health field his entire life, even in leadership, and you missed the signs. Maybe you are not equipped to lead."*

Then I heard the small still voice of the Holy Spirit say, *Trust in the LORD with all your heart, and lean not on your own understanding; in all your ways submit to Him, and He will make your paths straight.* (Proverbs 3:5-6).

As a child, I always felt so protected by my family; so many aunts, uncles, cousins and grandparents. I never worried about anyone bothering me or even thinking about bothering me. My cousins, aunts and uncles made sure we all knew how to fight and defend ourselves. Our family is huge; two sisters married two brothers. Mommy had nine siblings, and Daddy had 12 siblings. Mommy's eldest sister married my daddy's big brother.

I contacted my family and made them aware of what my son told me. There were family members who immediately stood with my son and me and who also wanted to hurt the abuser. There were others who said they stood with us, but whose actions showed otherwise as they still welcomed the predator and his mother into their space. Something I will never understand. Whose family is this? Surely, this is not the family I grew up in. I expected my entire family to show up and support my son and me the way I always showed up and supported everyone. The way that the family I grew up in always did.

There were many days I cried in silence with the knowledge of family members still accepting them into their space, aware of the abuse my son suffered. The betrayal I felt was unbearable. Did they not care about what message this sent to my son and to me? I was crushed. Many days and nights I cried and was in total disbelief. One night, I called my big little brother (I'm older than him, but he's just bigger than me in size.) screaming and crying because I saw pictures on social media of my cousin's birthday party, and the mother of the predator was there. They even brought food to the party! My brother had never heard or seen me like that in his entire life. I know it traumatized him. You see, I am the eldest. I am supposed to be the strong one.

Rage was building inside of me. I wanted to fly home to Buffalo and do damage. In that moment, my little brother allowed me to scream and cry it out, and he sat with me on the phone and talked me off the ledge. He encouraged me, and I stopped trying to make logic out of an illogical situation. My response to him in that moment was, *"I love you, little big brother! Thank you for creating space for me to be vulnerable."* I also thank God for my youngest aunt who has always been more like a big sister to me. She walked beside us and prayed us through one of the most difficult times of our lives. I love you and appreciate you more than you know. She has been one of my valley walkers my entire life.

Release them, forgive them, you must love them as I have commanded you to love. "What, God? Love them? "Do you not see what is happening? Do you not see how this is hurting my son and me? God, it's not fair!" *Release them, forgive them, you must love them as I have commanded you to love.* Overtime, I forgave them and I released them. I released them from what their titles meant in our family dynamic and the expectations that came with those titles. I had to for my sanity and peace. My soul depended on it. Familial relationships with some look different now - not in a bad way or where there is tension - and I am ok with that. I have forgiven them, and I am at peace. Forgiveness does not necessarily mean access or proximity.

Evil thrives in silence. Healing begins with truth! This revelation didn't happen in a vacuum. It came after years of grief, betrayal, and emotional exhaustion. I was already worn thin, but God, in His mercy, allowed truth to come forward, not to destroy us, but to begin the work of healing.

God showed so much grace and mercy during this time through the people HE placed in my life: my manager, who I affectionately call my brother from another mother and two of my co-workers who were also in leadership who I affectionately call my brother and sister. They carried me while at work. They were present for my team and me in so many ways. With no judgement, no questions asked, they covered me and loved me.

When my mind was in the clouds and on autopilot, they took hold of the throttle and landed the plane (my team). I love them, and I am forever grateful for them. My team was amazing as well. I loved my team. They all reminded me of how I always showed up for them, seeing them and being the best supervisor to them, and they performed at optimal level. You see, people remember how you show up and how you make them feel and return the favor in kind.

Later that same year, my mother-in-love passed away. We had the best mother/daughter relationship. She was truly my second mother in every sense of the relationship. Oh, how I miss her. She loved me as her daughter as if she gave birth to me, and she loved my sons as her grandsons. So much so, a friend of hers referred to our youngest son as her "step-grandson" while talking about her attendance at his basketball game. She responded with, *"Step? Who you stepping on? That's my grandson!"* Suffice to say, she never made that mistake again. Momma Vee loved her grandchildren with an unparalleled love - our five as we affectionately call them. High School theatre performances, dance recitals, piano recitals, soccer games, football and basketball games, she was always present whether she was feeling well or not.

When my mother-in-love passed away, I did not get to grieve her either. I did not get the luxury of falling apart or allowing myself to feel the huge void that was left when she went home to glory (heaven).

Again, I became the organizer, the planner, the strong one. The one who made the phone calls, managed the details, and held everyone else together.

There are moments in life when faith is no longer about having answers.

It becomes about holding onto God while everything inside you is screaming. That was one of those moments.

If you are reading this and carrying a truth you are afraid to speak, I want you to know you are not weak. You are courageous, and God is with you in every step of bringing what was hidden into the light. It's time to tell your truth and take back your power. Now is the time to heal. Seek counseling and know that God loves you so much, and so do I! Surrender your heart to HIM. I am so proud of you!

God is so faithful, he is a keeper of those that diligently seek him. My dearest Xavier, I am so proud of the man you are. Your courage, your strength, your fortitude. The work that you have put into your healing journey, allowing God into your heart, and honoring the yes that you gave God when you were just a child. I love watching you shine in your element, continuing to stand firm when faced with opposition. I always told you that you have such a beautiful mind. Oh, how I love you, Son, and I love what God has done and is doing in our relationship. I see you, and I hear you! Keep leaving it all on the stage.

Have I not commanded you? Be strong and courageous. Do not be afraid; do not be discouraged, for the LORD your God will be with you wherever you go (Joshua 1:9).

Chapter 6
The Unexpected Joy

I didn't go looking for joy. It found me.

In the middle of grief, betrayal, caregiving and exhaustion, God quietly placed something in my hands that I didn't even realize was a lifeline at the time. During COVID, when the world was closed, fear was loud, and isolation was heavy, God placed on my heart to start an online business that HE named Purposed Tees and More, LLC.

At first, it was simple.

Just shirts.
Just words.
Just Scripture. But God used it to keep me alive.

Every design I created was a declaration.
Every phrase was something I needed to believe.
Every order was a reminder that even in chaos, purpose still existed.

I wasn't just printing shirts, sweatshirts, and more. I was printing hope.

I was wearing God's Word on my chest when my heart felt fragile.

I was surrounding myself with truth when lies were trying to take root.

When everything else seemed out of control, this gave me something steady, something to hope for, something holy.

It was the first time in a long time that I felt a spark of joy that wasn't attached to survival. I would sit at my computer designing, praying, worshiping and creating. For a moment, *I could breathe.*

In this space of peace, like clockwork the enemy showed his head in the form of betrayal by someone I trusted with an idea God gave to me. Betrayal by someone you trust is a painful experience that will cause you to look at people differently and cause a wound that the enemy will use to gain access into your life if you do not forgive and release them. Understand, the assignment on your life is greater! *For if you forgive other people when they sin against you, your heavenly Father will also forgive you. But if you do not forgive others their sins, your father will not forgive your sins* (Matthew 6:14-15).

God was teaching me the importance of forgiveness and to use greater discernment knowing that what God has for you is for you! Release them, lay them at the feet of God and do not allow anger, resentment or bitterness to seep into your heart and change who God made you to be. *Above all else, guard your heart, for everything you do flows from it* (Proverbs 4:23). *Guard your heart Kia. There is work to do.*

You see, God knew what was coming for my body before I did, and he was equipping me with the solution.

HE knew how heavy the next season would be, and HE gave me joy before the storm.

My business wasn't just a creative outlet, it was a spiritual oxygen tank. It was and still is ministry. When grief, stress, betrayal and trauma were quietly taking their toll on my body, God had already placed something in my hands that kept me connected to HIM, to purpose, and to life.

God often hides our healing inside the trivial things we almost overlook.

Sometimes, joy is not loud. Sometimes, it comes as a whisper, the small still voice of the Holy Spirit reminding you of who God says you are and what HIS word says about you.

No temptation has overtaken you except what is common to mankind. And God is faithful; he will not let you be tempted beyond what you can bear. But when you are tempted, he will also provide a way out so that you can endure it (1 Corinthians 10:13-15).

PART III

Holding onto God
When You Feel Yourself Slipping

Chapter 7
When Your Own Soul Becomes the Battlefield

By the time the truth came out about my son, I had already been functioning on empty for a few years.

Grief from losing my Daddy.

The betrayal in my marriage.

The exhaustion of being strong for everyone else.

Now, the reality of my child having been abused.

Something inside me finally cracked.

I loved God. I still trusted Him, but there was a quiet war happening in my mind and in my heart. A war filled with questions I was afraid to speak and shame I didn't know how to release.

I kept replaying moments from my son's childhood. Words he had said and things I had brushed past. Innocent phrases that now sounded different and with every memory came the same cruel whisper:

You failed.
You should have known.
What kind of mother misses this?

Those thoughts didn't come from God, they came from the enemy (Satan), but they felt real.

I was a wife and a mother.

I am a leader, a mental health professional, and I felt disqualified.

I prayed. I cried. I tried to push those thoughts away - so many sleepless nights, so many nightmares - but they kept returning. Shame has a way of pretending to be truth when it's left unchallenged.

I didn't just need healing for what had happened. I needed healing from what I was telling myself about it.

God began to show me something I had never fully understood before. Trauma does not just wound the moment. It lodges itself in the soul creating holes in your soul, and when it's not released, it becomes a weight you carry everywhere you go.

I was carrying grief I never grieved.

Betrayal I never processed.

Pain I never named. And it was all piling up inside me.

This wasn't the end of my faith.

It was the beginning of a deeper one.

Chapter 8
Sitting In the Secret Place

When everything in my life felt unstable, God's Word became the one place that didn't move. My relationship with Christ was my solid foundation.

I didn't always have the strength to explain how I was feeling. Some days I couldn't even form the right prayers or words, but I could open my Bible. I could read. I could let God speak when I didn't have words of my own.

Scripture became more than something I studied.

It became something I held onto. I didn't realize how many Scriptures I knew until the enemy attacked me daily in my mind, in my sleep, and throughout the day.

Most mornings I would awaken tired - physically, emotionally, spiritually deep in my soul. I would reach for my Bible the way someone reaches for air. Not because I felt strong, but because I needed to survive.

Bible verses I had read my entire life suddenly meant something different. They weren't just something to memorize. They were personal. They became my reality.

I was angry, I was hurting, I was confused and I felt all alone. *"...Never will I leave you never will I forsake you (Hebrews 13:5).* I felt so lost with no sense of direction. Maybe my sons were better off without me. *"I will not die but live and will proclaim what the LORD has done. (Psalm 118:17).*

God, I had one job and I failed. I failed my sons. *For I know the plans I have for you, declares the LORD, plans to prosper you and not to harm you, plans to give you hope and a future (Jeremiah 29:11).*

God, did I hear you correctly, was I supposed to marry my husband? I must have heard you wrong. God, he committed adultery! *The Lord makes firm the steps of the one who delights in him (Psalm 37:23)*

God, the weight of it all is too heavy. I don't want to carry it anymore. *"Cast all your anxiety on him because he cares for you (1 Peter 5:7).*

The Lord is close to the brokenhearted (Psalm 34:18).

I was brokenhearted, and He was close.

He heals the broken in heart and binds up their wounds (Psalm 147:3).

I needed binding, I was coming undone. I needed care. I needed to know that God sees me.

I wasn't walking around the valley, I was in the loneliest, deepest, darkest valley, and God was there, too.

Some days all I could do was read one verse repeatedly.

Other days I would write them down and place them on my bathroom mirror.

I wore them, I spoke them, I breathed them.

When my thoughts were loud, God's Word was louder and slowly, quietly, faithfully... it was all that was holding me together.

Even though I walk through the darkest valley, I will fear no evil, for you are with me; your rod and your staff, they comfort me. (Psalm 23:4).

Chapter 9
How to Pray When You're Too Tired to Pray

There were seasons when prayer felt easy, when words flowed, when worship rose, and when faith felt light. Then there were seasons when all I could do was sit in God's presence and breathe.

Pain has a way of stealing language. When grief, betrayal, fear, and exhaustion pile up, you don't always know what to say. Sometimes you don't even know what you feel. You just know that everything hurts.

In those moments, I learned something sacred:

God does not require polished prayers.

He wants honest ones.

Some of my prayers were nothing more than, "God, it's me, and Jesus, Help Me."

Some were tears, some were silent, and some were worship songs playing softly in the background while I lay on the floor.

I didn't have to impress HIM. I didn't have to smile through the pain, the loneliness, the grief.

I just had to show up. I began to understand that prayer wasn't about saying the right thing, it was about staying connected to my LORD and Savior when I didn't have strength left.

There were days I would open my Bible and let Scripture pray for me. There were nights I would play worship music and let God minister to my heart while I rested, and through it all, God was still listening.

If you are in a season where prayer feels heavy or impossible, I want you to know this: you don't have to perform for God. He knows your pain, and even when you don't have the words, He hears you, HE sees you, HE sees your tears.

Faith is not proven by how beautifully you pray. It's proven by the fact that you keep coming back staying at the feet of God and surrendering your heart to HIM.

The eyes of the Lord are toward the righteous and his ears are attentive to their cry (Psalm 34:15).

Chapter 10
Choosing Faith Over Feelings

There is a version of faith that feels warm and reassuring, the kind you have when life is good and prayers are being answered quickly. Then there is the kind of faith that must be chosen.

Chosen when you are tired.
Chosen when you are disappointed.
Chosen when you don't understand what God is doing.

This was the faith I learned in the fire.

I didn't always feel hopeful.
I didn't always feel strong.
I didn't always feel like God was near, but I knew that He was.

Some days my choice looked like reading one verse.

Some days it looked like worshiping through tears.

Some days it looked like simply getting out of bed and saying, *"Jesus, Help Me."*

Faith is not the absence of doubt.

It is the decision to trust God in the presence of it.

Even when my marriage was fractured.
Even when my family was hurting.
Even when my body began to fail me.
Even when grief was heavy.

I kept choosing HIM.

Not because I understood everything, but because I knew who HE was, and little by little, that choice kept me anchored while everything else was shifting.

"Whoever dwells in the shelter of the Most High will rest in the shadow of the Almighty. I will say of the Lord, "He is my refuge and my fortress, my God, in whom I trust (Psalm 91:1-2)."

PART IV

There's Another in the Fire

Chapter 11
What I Learned About God in the Dark

When my body began to fail, I realized something that took me by surprise. I wasn't just fighting sickness. I was fighting everything I had been holding inside for the past six years. My soul was wounded and in need of healing.

By 2021, I could barely breathe without feeling winded. Walking up the stairs felt like climbing a mountain. Standing to cook or shower left me exhausted. By the time I finished getting dressed and doing my hair, I felt like I had just run a marathon. I noticed that my skin took on a grayish tint that I covered with makeup, and slowly my body was betraying me.

One day, while sitting on my computer working on my business, I started bleeding from my nose so badly that clots were falling. My husband and our youngest son rushed me to the same hospital where my mother-in-love had passed away in September of 2019. Because of COVID, they couldn't come inside to accompany me. My baby boy sat in the car crying, begging me to promise him that I would come back out. I promised him that I would and for the first time on the inside, I felt afraid, *"LORD, would I be coming back out?"*

Seeing the fright and hearing it in our youngest son's voice made me pause and really reflect on how all that has happened was affecting him. I had been running on auto pilot for the past several years, and I did not see how traumatized he was with all that was happening. He was feeling everything that was happening within our family. He was the one that was always up under me, so he noticed everything.

He lost his Papa (my Daddy), and he watched his Nana grieve his Papa and wanted to take her pain away, all while missing his Papa too. He lost his Grandma Vee. He was the grandchild with me at every one of her doctor's appointments and every hospital stays. He was watching his big brother who he loves dearly and looks up to relive one of the most painful times of his life, which caused him to distance himself from us all. He was watching his bonus Dad (my husband) grieve the loss of his Mom, all while pulling away from everyone. Now his rock, his Mommy, was walking into the same hospital that we walked his Grandma Vee into, and she never walked back out.

I was told I would require surgery to stop the nosebleed. I prayed and put a demand on the word of God, Isaiah 53:5 to be exact, *"But he was pierced for our transgressions, he was crushed for our iniquities; the punishment that brought us peace was on him, and by his wounds we are healed."* I walked out of the hospital more than three and a half hours later with no surgery required. God stopped the nosebleed.

Oh Hunter, my sweet baby boy, please forgive me. I held him so tight and slept alongside him that night when I was discharged.

Later that year, the day before my birthday in December, I ended up in the emergency room again, thinking I was having a heart attack. I awoke on my birthday in the hospital after a battery of tests. The doctors said the pain in my chest that I thought was a heart attack was induced by stress. My cardiologist looked at my husband and me straight in the eye and said, *"Whatever it is, you need to let it go. You're too young for this."* Then my cardiologist went and got me a balloon for my birthday, something the nurses were surprised about and said that they had never seen that side of him. God shows up in so many ways letting you know that He sees you and that He loves you.

In January of 2022, my primary care physician gave a diagnosis I was not prepared to hear, one which impacted my lungs and heart that was becoming progressively worse as it was in an advanced stage. I asked if there was surgery or medicine that I could take to heal me. He said there was no cure, and unfortunately, it was a medical condition unto death. I heard him, BUT I knew God! Not only did I know God, but I also believed HIS Word and began to declare his Word over my life. My go to Scripture was, *"But he was pierced for our transgressions, he was crushed for our iniquities; the punishment that brought us peace was on him, and by his wounds we are healed (Isaiah 53:5)"*

I told the doctor, *"You're going to see a miracle up close and personal. God is reversing this."* He smiled, but I could see sadness in his eyes. He expressed that he knew my faith was strong. He had no idea! People are always watching you, even when you don't realize it. Every place that you show up is your platform, the place where you demonstrate Christ in your actions, behavior and what you speak because we represent HIM. *"So, God created mankind in his own image, in the image of God he created them; male and female he created them (Genesis 1:27)."*

I never came into agreement with the diagnosis, meaning I never said I have it. I always said, the diagnosis given.... You see, stating that I have would mean that I was coming into agreement with the diagnosis. *"The tongue has the power of life and death, and those who love it will eat it's fruit (Proverbs 18:21)."* Everything I refused to feel had been finding a way to express itself in my body. I walked to my car and that's when I cried out to God from a place deeper than I have ever before. I was angry, I was confused, *"God have, I not been through enough. God, I don't understand, why me!"*

I was tired and, during that time, God showed me something that changed everything.

He showed me that the bitterness, anger, grief, betrayal, and unforgiveness I had been carrying since 2016 had become a weight on my soul, a doorway, a point of entry giving the enemy access to my body. *"For the wages of sin is death, but the gift of God is eternal life in Christ Jesus our Lord* (Romans 6:23)."

Despite what I was feeling, all the tests, the setbacks and limitations over that year, I held onto and declared the Scriptures over my life, specifically Isaiah 53:5. I chose to walk by faith and not by sight. I chose to live and not die and declare the promises of God over my life. God led me into a true season of forgiveness, not just for others, but also for myself.

As I began to release the pain, grief, humiliation, anger, bitterness, rage, resentment, and expectations of people who came with titles, over that next year, something began to change. My color slowly returned. My breath came back. I could walk without pain or feeling like my heart was going to burst through my chest while my lungs felt as if they were on fire. I could walk and run our subdivision again. Something that I could not do for the past two years! I could live again. God healed more than my heart, mind and body. HE healed my soul and made me whole!

Chapter 12
God Is Close to the Broken Hearted

Feeling broken does not mean you are finished.

I learned that in the most intimate way possible - in doctor's offices, in prayer closets, and in the quiet moments when only God and I knew how afraid I really was.

After months of tests, fear, and exhaustion, something remarkable happened.

As I forgave.

As I released.

As I laid down what I had been carrying and left it at the feet of God...

My body began to respond.

I started breathing without struggling.

I could climb stairs again.

I could stand, cook, laugh, live, and when I went back to my doctors - the cardiologist, the pulmonologist, and my primary care physician - they found no evidence of what had once been labeled "unto death."

The diagnosis was gone! The God who heals did it again!

My medical records were updated! I received my papers in the mail! Glory to God, Jesus healed me! You see, Isaiah 53:5 (NIV) tells us *that, "...But he was pierced for our transgressions, he was crushed for our iniquities; the punishment that brought us peace was on him, and by his wounds we are healed."* This was a Scripture I kept on my mirror and declared and believed daily regardless of how I was feeling, regardless of what the tests showed, or regardless of what the medical records showed.

My body was healed!

In February of 2023, I was told I was in perfect health.

That was not medicine. That was the blood of Jesus, God's grace and mercy, and the Word of God in action!

God showed me that I may have been wounded but not defeated. Pressed, but not crushed. The fire did not take me out. It refined me.

Chapter 13
When Love Is Restored

There was a time when I didn't believe our marriage could be healed. To be honest, I did not want it anymore.

Too much had happened.
Too much had been broken.
Too much pain lived between us.

During my healing journey, my husband and I separated. Not out of anger, but out of necessity. We both needed space for God to do His work in us without the noise of resentment, fear, and old wounds.

God didn't just heal my body. He went after our hearts.

While I was in the secret place with God, forgiving others and being healed, God was working on my husband, too. In ways I could not see. You see, the affair was never about me, it was about him, his brokenness that only God could mend once he surrendered his heart to Him. Many times, the spouse who is cheated on wonders what they could have done differently, why was their love not enough, or what was missing. The answer is nothing. Infidelity is a choice not a mistake. He took accountability and called it what it was, a selfish choice, as my husband would later admit in therapy.

We didn't come back together because things got easier.

We came back together because God made us new. You see, marriage is ministry. It is a covenant, not just between you and your spouse, but between, God, you and your spouse. When God brought you together, he brought you together for kingdom purpose. Covenant with your spouse and God is sacred. It's powerful, and the enemy (Satan) hates covenant between husband and wife. *"Though one may be overpowered, two can defend themselves. A cord of three strands is not quickly broken* (Ecclesiastes 4:12)."

We learned how to pray together. How to worship together. How to speak honestly. How to forgive deeply.

We are not the same people we used to be, and that is the miracle.

We renewed our wedding vows in August 2023 because our original covenant had been broken. We invited God back into our marriage. Our marriage is not perfect, but it is healed, and it is holy. We did the work individually and together. Our circle interceded for us, ministered to us, and prayed for us. They held us accountable and to God's word. They did not judge; they loved us through it.

God allowed us to minister to other married couples and those in relationships looking to be married. We were able to draw from places in our marriage where we recognized that we allowed the enemy in and did not always keep God as the priority in our marriage. We discussed the importance of keeping God at the center of marriage and understanding that marriage is ministry; it's kingdom work.

If God could restore us after betrayal, grief, separation, and the fire the enemy thought would consume us, HE can restore what feels impossible in your life, too. My valley walkers knew something that my emotions at the time would not allow me to see. God was not finished with us yet. He still had purpose for this marriage, this union, and our family, and they interceded for us. God gave us something beautiful from the ashes.

"Therefore, what God has joined together, let no one separate (Mark 10:9)."

Chapter 14
Forgiving While in The Fire

"Then Peter came to Jesus and asked, "Lord, how many times shall I forgive my brother or sister who sins against me? Up to seven times?" Jesus answered, "I tell you, not seven times, but seventy-seven times. (Matthew 18:21-22)."

Forgiving didn't erase my memories.

I still remember the passing of my father, and my mother-in-love.
I still remember the betrayal.
I still remember my son's courage.
I still remember the fear, the hospitals, the diagnosis, the waiting rooms, and the prayers. But, those people, situations, and memories no longer consume me.

Forgiving didn't make those experiences disappear. It gave me my breath back while I told it. It became my living, breathing testimony of God's love, faithfulness, healing, grace, mercy, deliverance and redemption. You see, God did not just heal me; HE made me whole!

For a long time, I thought forgiveness meant pretending things didn't hurt. I thought it meant minimizing what happened. I thought it meant being okay with what was never okay.

Forgiveness is not agreement.

It is release! It is a peace that surpasses all understanding.

It is saying, *"I will not let this pain live inside me anymore."*

When I forgave them, I released them all! Letting go meant releasing the power those wounds held over my life, the strongholds. In releasing them went the expectations I had of the people who held titles in my life. I had to learn to stop expecting others to show up the way I would. To stop expecting me from others, what we often label as reciprocity, when they lack the capacity or wherewithal to show up in the same manner that I do.

The hardest part in forgiving was learning to forgive myself. Forgiving myself for missing the signs and not protecting my son, for not realizing at the time how much my youngest son was hurting, too, for allowing others to get too close, for being angry with myself, for feeling foolish and not retaliating in a manner that my flesh was screaming to.

Something beautiful and sacred happened when I chose to finally forgive myself. In that moment, it was as if Jesus himself opened HIS arms, held me, and allowed me to release it all. It was then that the shame lifted, the heaviness went away, I could finally breath, and my heart found its new rhythm - the rhythm that Abba (God as father) always intended for me to have, which is to be in sync with HIM.

I finally saw myself not as a woman who failed, but as a woman who survived, one who is deeply loved and seen by God.

God didn't heal me so I could pretend nothing happened. He healed me so that I could walk in the purpose which I was created to do. Understand, God created each of us with a plan, and HIS plan is perfect! Even though the path at times seemed unbearable, I still trusted God's plan. *"For I know the plans I have for you,"* declares the Lord, *"plans to prosper you and not to harm you, plans to give you hope and a future (Jeremiah 29:11).*

The enemy could no longer use those wounds that punctured my soul to keep me in bondage, in anger, bitterness, resentment, and sometimes rage. I could now walk in the purpose HE created me to walk in because I chose to forgive and allowed God to heal those soul wounds. I can be the wife, mother, minister and leader I was created to be. I am created in God's image, and the feelings that I carried during that time was not a reflection of HIM. The more I released people and circumstances and chose to do the work starting with forgiveness, I could feel God healing me from the inside out, and what HE was doing internally began to show outwardly. *"So, God created mankind in his own image, in the image of God he created them; male and female he created them (Genesis 1:27)."*

I also learned that forgiveness does not always mean reconciliation or even access. What forgiveness does mean is that we are to love the way that God commanded us to, and sometimes love is wishing them well and that they, too, would accept Jesus Christ as their personal LORD and Savior. *"My command is this, love each other as I have loved you. (John 15:12)."*

Release those who have hurt you in any way, and lay them at the feet of Jesus. Surrender your heart and those wounds to Jesus, and allow Him to heal you and make you whole.

PART V

For the Reader Still in the Flames

Chapter 15
If You Are Hurting Right Now

If you are holding this book with shaking hands, I want you to know something before you read another word:

You are not weak.
You are not broken beyond repair.
You are not forgotten.

You are hurting and that matters.

You may be grieving a loss no one else sees.
You may be living with betrayal that still stings.
You may be carrying memories that won't let you sleep.
You may be trying to believe God while your heart feels tired and you feel like giving up.

I wrote this book for you.

Not to give you easy answers.

Not to rush your healing, but to remind you that you are not alone in the fire.

God sees you where you are not where you think you should be.

You don't have to have it all together to come to HIM. You don't have to be strong today. You don't have to know what tomorrow looks like. You don't have to come with an elaborate prayer. Open your mouth and begin to speak your heart and invite HIM in.

Just keep breathing and keep believing that even here, even now, God is still with you because HE promised to never leave nor forsake you.

I encourage you to pull out your Bible and read Psalm 91. Get in the secret place with HIM, and cry out to Abba, because HE loves you and HE cares about everything concerning you.

Chapter 16
How to Hold onto God
When You Feel Like You're Drowning

There were moments in my life when faith felt like the only thing keeping my head above water.

Not because everything was okay, but because everything wasn't.

When you are drowning emotionally, spiritually, or even physically, you don't need complicated answers. You need something solid to hold onto.

Here is what held me:

I stopped pretending I was fine.
I told God the raw truth, and I did not hold back.
I let Him see the parts of me that were angry, afraid, broken and exhausted.

I created sacred space; I created a space in my bedroom for just me and Jesus, the secret place. (Psalm 91). I dwelt in the secret place with HIM. Some may create a prayer closet, or another room in your home. I created this space in my bedroom. It was an area in the corner of my bedroom where I would sit or lay, listen to worship music, read my Bible, pray, cry out to God, throw tantrums (Yes tantrums. God is My father *"Abba."*) and just sit and listen. I encourage you to create a secret place in your home for you and God, invite HIM in. I promise you that HE will meet you there.

Sometimes it was worship music in the car or in the shower. It's something about praise and worship in the shower, crying out to God as the water purifies; cleanses. There were many times I was the woman in the dramatic seen in a movie that broke down crying in the shower.... She was me and I was her.

Sometimes it was just sitting still and letting God speak. I kept a journal and wrote what I was feeling and what I heard the Holy Spirit whisper to me.

I stayed connected to HIM through HIS Word.

Not perfectly, but persistently.

I forgave over and again. I said it out loud, called out names and situations until what was coming out of my mouth resonated in my heart.

Not because it was easy, but because my life depended on it. My soul, the souls of my children, and my purpose was at stake. You see, I would be and am the repairer of the breach for my bloodline. I am one of the generational curse breakers for our bloodline. I encourage you to be the person in your family that says, "This ran in our family, until it ran into me. By the power and authority given to me through Christ Jesus, it is broken off our bloodline!"

When I struggled to believe, I leaned on God's faithfulness instead. I had to remind myself of God's résumé in my life, how HE always showed up, how HE never left me, how HE protected me and kept me in my darkest hours, and how I may have bent, but HE never allowed me to break! He is a Keeper!

If you feel like you are barely surviving right now, hear this: God loves you, He sees you, and He's waiting on you to invite Him into your life. God will meet you where you are.

Chapter 17
The Fire Will Not Consume You

There is a truth I need you to carry with you long after you close this book:

What you are walking through will not destroy you.

The fire was never meant to take you out, but to refine and purify you.

It was meant to reveal what was already inside of you - faith, strength, resilience, and a God who never left your side.

I know what it feels like to wonder if you're going to make it. I know what it feels like to be tired of being strong. I know what it feels like to love God and still feel overwhelmed by life.

I also know what it feels like to stand on the other side of the fire and realize...

You're still here.

God did not abandon you in the flames. There was ALWAYS another in the fire and HIS name is Jesus. *"Look, I see four men walking around in the fire, unbound and unharmed, and the fourth looks like a son of the gods* (Daniel 3:25)."

Jesus was there, holding you, refining you, and carrying you when you couldn't walk on your own. When you felt like giving up; when you felt as if you no longer wanted to be here, Jesus was there.

If you are reading this and you feel like everything is burning around you, remember this:

The fire does not get the final word. God does, and HE is not finished with you! So, when the flames seem high, when life seems unbearable, call on the fourth man in the fire. His name is Jesus. Accept him as your personal LORD and Savior. HE will never leave nor forsake you!

If you have not accepted Jesus as your personal LORD and Savior, I encourage you to surrender your heart to him today and receive a love like no other! Open your Bible and make this declaration out loud because Romans 10:9 tells us, *"If you declare with your mouth, "Jesus is Lord," and believe in your heart that God raised him from the dead, you will be saved."*

Jesus answered, "I am the way and the truth and the life. No one comes to the Father except through me (John 14:6)."

SPECIAL CHAPTER

Chapter 18

When I learned of the abuse my son endured, I could not accurately put into words at that time all that I was feeling, but God knew. In a conversation with one of my valley walkers (my sister-friend in Christ) she was at work and cried out to God in anger, in pain and disbelief at what he had experienced. This is what God said to her, and she pinned it.

A Letter to Xavier

Dear Xavier,

The greatest trick the devil ever pulled was convincing the world that he didn't exist.

So, in your unexplainable pain and suffering you assume I wasn't in the midst.

Your adversary wants you traveling in the worldly wilderness lost and confused, circling mountains labeled abused.

You didn't know how to articulate what was being perpetuated. Yet you spoke loud and clearly in fear. Out of lewd selfishness you were not heard, that is a truth that will remain absurd.

You were in a circle where ears turned deaf, eyes turned blind, aged people were evicted from their minds, and none of this was my design. A tenacious immunity was built into such a vile lifestyle. People were mute to your pain for their unwarranted gain.

You're fearfully and wonderfully made; your adversary the trickster would use that against you to make you feel self – betrayed. At times when you were being manipulated by inordinate affection, you were resilient and uncovered yourself to strategically cover others compassionately with child-like protection.

It's safe to reside within me outside of your head, so many of the lies visiting can permanently be put to bed. With practice over time, you will adapt to a healed, renewed mind.

You spoke your truth now walk free from the binding noose. You are the apple of my eyes this is one reason why your purpose was being disguised.... Remember the failed attempt at suicide? You have work to do, that's why your adversary wants your vision misconstrued.

Will you meet me at the crossroads? Allow me to assist you in unpacking your cumbersome loads.

I know you feel that while you were in pain I slept, that's the furthest thing from the truth I wept. I preserved you; I knew you would come to your moment of truth.

Memories, feelings and emotions you no longer have to suppress come to me, I promise you will find peace, comfort and rest.

Your identity isn't going to be found outside of me, although I have declared you free. You didn't just survive, you thrived. The things I have in store for your life may take you by surprise.

I've been distorted my true identity through the lenses of pain by many have been aborted.

I make all things new; you can be reborn and all the broken places can be reformed.

The venom that's been spewed are deflections; it's truly others self-reflections.

I am not the author of confusion; your adversary wants you in a constant state of delusion.

Your adversary wants you anxious and manic, crippled by panic. I want you anxious for nothing, whole, healed set free, deliberately leaning on me.

If the heinous actions you lived through were a generational curse, no longer does it have to be rehearsed right now it's being broken and reversed. You will no longer unwillingly be chronically exposed to that which is perverse.

There's nothing new under the sun, your adversary is a liar, murderer and a thief, and he now has your mother wallowing in grief. No worries, I'm going to be her peace and release.

Listen, your mother would walk nude in a desert on scalding coals before she would ever willingly throw you in a fire to be tormented and receive lacerations to your soul.

I'm going to walk you through this, of course not against your will; it's already paid for all you need to do is be still.

Your adversary wants to victim shame and victim blame, he doesn't have any new ploys, so he plays on trauma like he's playing with new toys.

In a hyper – sexualized culture predators relentlessly prey, not having in mind that there is no expiration date to judgement day.

You have the nail to this coffin, this is a giant that you spoke to and slayed, I've equipped you with the power to bury this and make death behave.

I'm not asking that you have a traditional or contemporary relationship with me. I'm asking that you would have a personal one; after all you are my son! I'm not confined to a building, I'm wherever you are. I know I may seem out of reach but truly I'm always with you, I'm never far.

Your adversary wanted you condemned; he wanted you carrying unbearable secrets to your grave. He wanted past events to be your current slave.

Evil, calamity, devastation and destruction have always been calculated to disprove my existence, so I understand your resistance.

Here's the twist in all of this, your adversary and I both exist. Humanity has free will, they get to decide how they will travel for life's ride.

Like the rose that grew from concrete you have the power to rise from what was meant to be defeat.

Until we meet face to face, trust the process and believe you will be met with grace.

Love Your Father – God

Created By: Shawntrice Amelia Green - 3/18/2019.

Isaiah 43:19 (NIV) – *"See, I am doing a new thing! Now it springs up; do you not perceive it? I am making a way in the wilderness and streams in the wasteland."*

Chapter 19
To My Valley Walkers
(My Sisters-Friends in Christ)

Hey Sis...There is a kind of love that only reveals itself in the dark.

When the fire was raging around me. When grief, betrayal, illness and heartbreak were louder than my own voice. When I did not have the words to pray and articulate what I needed in those moments, God sent me women who didn't run and who are still here. Women who didn't judge. Women who didn't try to fix me or rush me.

They stayed. They prayed when I couldn't find the words.

They listened when my heart was too heavy to carry it alone. The times I screamed and cried in pain, grief and sorrow.

They sat with me when silence was all I had. They showed up when I went silent.

They believed for me when my faith was tired.

These were my *valley walkers*; my circle of sister-friends who met me in the lowest places and never made me feel small for being there.

They didn't ask me to be strong.
They didn't shame me for bending.
They didn't need me to perform.

They covered me when I felt naked and exposed. They shielded me.

In my darkest seasons, they reminded me of who I am and what God says about me. They spoke life over me when I was tempted to give up. They held my hands, wiped my tears, and prayed heaven down on my behalf. There were no pity parties. They loved me with an accountability that I desperately needed.

They prayed for me in private and openly.

They called and sent a text at just the right time.

They showed up with no explanation, just love.

They were and still are God's gift to me. Your circle truly matters!

My healing would not look the way it does without you.

To every person who walked with me through the fire...

Thank you for not leaving.
Thank you for believing.
Thank you for loving me through it all.

You were the hands and feet of God when I needed HIM most.

I love you infinitely, and I am Forever grateful!

Kia

Epilogue

Still Standing. Still Believing. Still Here.

I didn't come through the fire unchanged. I came through it awakened.

There are things I will always carry - memories, lessons, scars that tell the story of where I've been - but those scars no longer define me. They testified that I survived what was meant to break me.

I am still standing.

Not because I was strong but because God was faithful.

I am still believing.

Not because I have all the answers, but because I know who holds them, and I am still here.

Here to love.
Here to serve.
Here to testify that even in the darkest places, God's light still reaches us.

If you are reading this and you are in your own fire, I want you to know something with certainty:

Your story is not over.
Your pain is not wasted.
And your faith, even if it feels small right now, is enough.

God meets us in the ashes and turns them into something holy.

And just like me...

You will rise.

A Letter to My Sons

My precious Xavier and Hunter,

My heart in human form. There are so many things I want to tell you both, but words never seem big enough to hold a mother's heart. You have watched me walk through fire. You have seen me tired, afraid, praying, fighting, believing, and sometimes just trying to make it through another day and still, you loved me and showed me so much grace.

I want you to know something with every part of you: I am so proud of you, and I am so happy God chose me to be your mom! You both were my motivation to keep going, to keep fighting, to keep showing up. You are my invaluable gift from the LORD.

I am so proud of the courage it takes to speak truth. I am so proud of the strength it takes to survive, and I am so proud of the Man and young man you both are and becoming.

You are seen.
You are cherished.
You are deeply loved by God and by me.

No matter where life takes you, know this: you come from a woman who prayed for you, fights for you, and believes in you more than words can say.

Loving you Forever,
Your mom, Kia

A Letter to God

Abba Father,

I don't even know where to begin.

You saw me when no one else did (El Roi-The God That Sees).

You heard my prayers when they didn't come out as words.

You held me when I was too tired to hold myself.

You stayed.

When I was grieving.
When I was betrayed.
When my child was hurting.
When my body was breaking.
When my faith was tired.

You never left.

I didn't always understand You.

I didn't always like what was happening, but I always knew You were with me.

Thank You for walking me through the fire instead of around it.

Thank You for healing what I didn't even know how to name.

Thank You for giving me my breath back in my body and in my soul.

Everything I am now because You didn't give up on me..

I love you!
Love, your daughter, Kia

A Letter to the Woman or Man in the Fire

To every Woman or Man reading this who feels tired, broken, or overwhelmed...

I see you.

I see the way you hold everyone else together while quietly falling apart and the prayers you pray through tears. I see the strength it takes to keep showing up when life keeps knocking you down.

You don't have to be perfect to be powerful.
You don't have to be healed to be hopeful.
You don't have to have it all together to be held by God.

If you are in the fire right now, remember this:

Fire refines; it does not erase.

You are still here for a reason.

Your story is still being written, and God is not finished with you yet.

Hold on. Better days are coming.

With love and faith, Kia

Moments With God
(what is God revealing to you in this moment)

Moments With God
(what is God revealing to you in this moment)

Moments With God
(what is God revealing to you in this moment)

About the Author

Kia Luster is a wife, mother, minister, entrepreneur, and purpose-driven leader whose life and work are rooted in Jesus Christ, healing, and community. Originally from Buffalo, New York, and now residing in Charlotte, North Carolina, Kia is known for her authentic voice, compassionate leadership, and unwavering belief in the power of God to restore what has been broken.

She is the visionary behind Hey Sis, Sisterhood on a Kingdom Level Ministries, a faith-based community dedicated to uplifting, empowering and uniting women through spiritual growth, emotional healing, and authentic connection. Kia is also the founder of Purposed Tees and More, LLC, a faith forward apparel and merchandise brand created to boldly declare God's Word, speak life, and remind people of their divine purpose.

Through her ministry, business, and now her writing, Kia's mission is clear: to lead others to Jesus Christ; helping them find hope, healing, and clarity amid life's hardest seasons.

"Faith Through the Fire" is her first book, a testimony of resilience, redemption, and the faithfulness of God through grief, betrayal, trauma, and healing.

You can stay connected and learn more about Kia, her ministry, and her business at:

Website: www.KiaLuster.com
E-mail: lusterkia@gmail.com